WORLD WAR I

Lisa Zamosky & Maci Reed

Consultant

Jennifer M. Lopez, NBCT, M.S.Ed.
Teacher Specialist—History/Social Studies
Office of Curriculum & Instruction
Norfolk Public Schools

Publishing Credits

Rachelle Cracchiolo, M.S.Ed., *Publisher*
Conni Medina, M.A.Ed., *Editor in Chief*
Emily R. Smith, M.A.Ed., *Content Director*
Véronique Bos, *Creative Director*
Robin Erickson, *Art Director*
Michelle Jovin, M.A., *Associate Editor*
Mindy Duits, *Senior Graphic Designer*

Image Credits: front cover, p.1 Galerie Bilderwelt/Getty Images; pp.4–5 State Library of New South Wales; p.5 (right) Library of Congress [LC-USZC4-11303]; p.6 (left), pp.22–23 Cassowary Colorizations; pp.6–7 (bottom) LOC [LC-DIG-ppmsc-09309]; p.7 (top) Bianchetti/Leemage; p.8 (top) Newscom; p.9 (l) New York Evening World; p.9 (r) LOC [LC-DIG-ggbain-26204]; p.10 (l), pp.12–13 (bottom) National Library of Scotland; p.10 (r) LOC [LC-DIG-ggbain-17676]; pp.10–11 (bottom) LOC [2007661941]; p.11 (top), pp.14–15, p.32 (l) Everett Historical/Shutterstock; p.13 (l) Susan Law Cain/Shutterstock; p.14 (l) Robert Hunt Picture Library; p.14 (r) LOC [LC-DIG-ppmsca-51295]; p.16 Woodrow Wilson Presidential Library Archives; p.17 (l) LOC [LC-DIG-acd-2a06155]; p.17 (r) Corbis via Getty Images; p.18 New York National Guard; 19 (l), p.21, p.23 (top), p.28 , p.29 (all) U.S. National Archives; p.19 (r) John D. Kisch/Separate Cinema Archive/Getty Images; p.20 (l) Viktor Karlovich Bulla; p.20 (top r) LOC [LC-USZC4-2950]; p.20 (bottom r) LOC [LC-DIG-ggbain-24573]; p.22 Bettmann/Getty Images; p.23 (bottom) LOC [LC-USZC4-1421]; p.24 (l) LOC [LC-USZ62-30948]; p.24 (r) Gilder Lehrman Collection; p.25 Imperial War Museum; p.27 (top) Deutsches Bundesarchiv; p.27 (bottom l) Julius Jääskeläinen/Flickr; p.27 (bottom r) LOC, Rare Book and Special Collections Division [192.00.00]; p.32 (r) LOC [LC-USZC4-8055]; all other images from Shutterstock.

Library of Congress Cataloging-in-Publication Data
Names: Zamosky, Lisa, author. | Reed, Maci, author.
Title: World War I / Lisa Zamosky & Maci Reed.
Description: 1st. | Huntington Beach : Teacher Created Materials, 2019. | Audience: Age 7. | Audience: Grades 2-3 | Summary: "World War I was one of the most devastating conflicts in human history. Millions of people were killed or wounded during the four years of war. The war was so shocking that people thought it would never happen again. However, the effects of the war would lead to another worldwide battle just a few decades later. This is the story of the so-called "Forgotten War.""-- Provided by publisher.
Identifiers: LCCN 2019024309 (print) | LCCN 2019024310 (ebook) | ISBN 9781425850661 (paperback) | ISBN 9781425850661 (ebook)
Subjects: LCSH: World War, 1914-1918--Juvenile literature.
Classification: LCC D522.7 .Z36 2019 (print) | LCC D522.7 (ebook) | DDC 940.3--dc23
LC record available at https://lccn.loc.gov/2019024309
LC ebook record available at https://lccn.loc.gov/2019024310

TCM Teacher Created Materials
5301 Oceanus Drive
Huntington Beach, CA 92649-1030
www.tcmpub.com
ISBN 978-1-4258-5066-1

Printed in China 51497

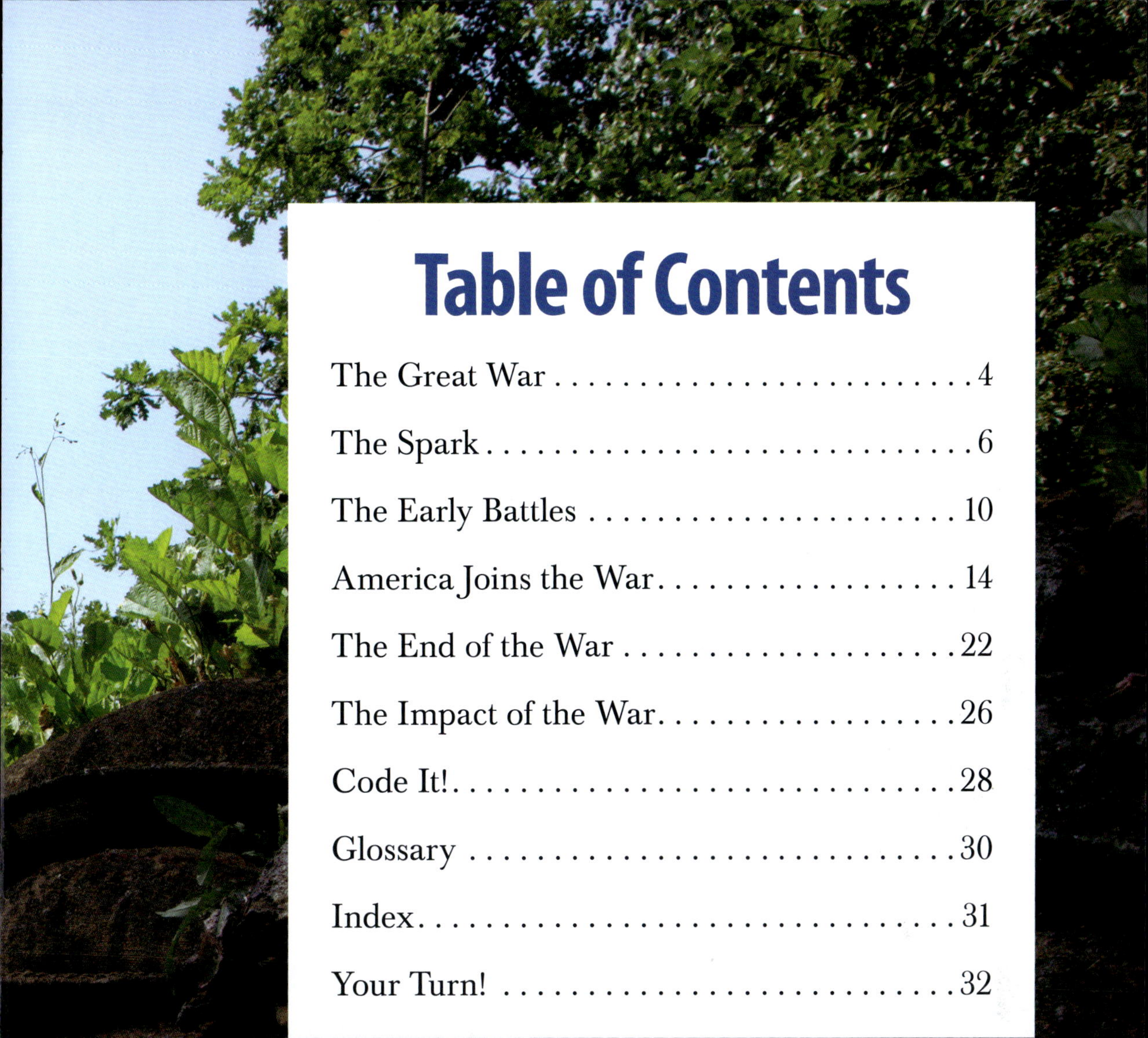

Table of Contents

The Great War

In 1914, a war began in Europe. At the time, people called it the Great War. More nations battled in this war than in any other war before it. A total of 65 million soldiers fought over the course of four years. Millions of people died. It is one of the largest human tragedies the world has ever seen. Today, this war is called World War I.

The problems that caused this war had been developing for quite some time. Some European countries were becoming very rich and their populations were growing. As a result, they wanted to take over more land. These countries had large armies and navies. However, they still needed support from other countries. Many countries signed agreements with each other that said they would go to war if one of their allies, or partners, were attacked.

The world was changing. All it would take was one event to send the world to war.

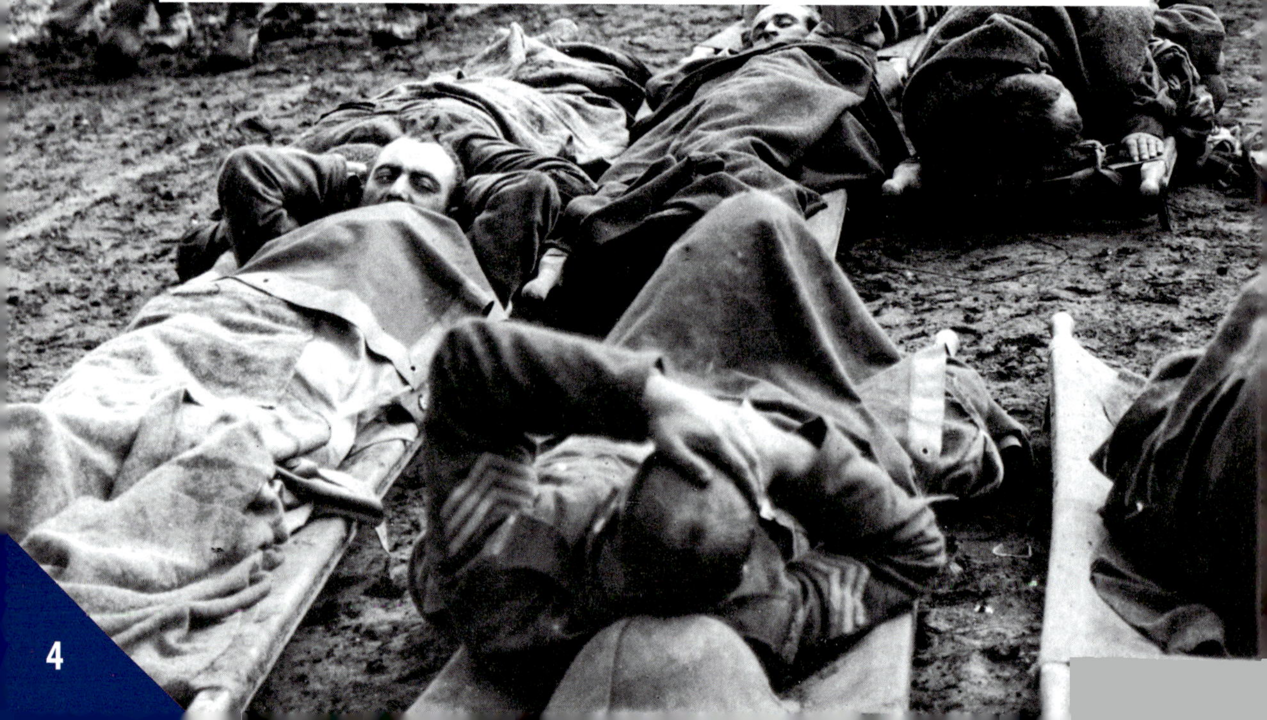

Building Up Forces

At the start of the war, Germany had more than eight million soldiers in its army. Russia had four million soldiers; France had three million soldiers. Great Britain had spent hundreds of years building up its Royal Navy. When the war began, the Royal Navy had more ships than the next two largest navies combined.

To End All Wars

People thought that by fighting a big war, they could have a peaceful future. They believed that no one would want another worldwide war. So, they also called World War I the "War to End All Wars."

The Spark

In the years before the war began, there were conflicts in eastern Europe. Serbia and Bosnia used to be part of the Ottoman Empire. They had fought for independence. However, there was a new threat. Slowly, the Austro-Hungarian Empire was moving into parts of Bosnia.

Some Serbian people wanted Bosnians to fight the invasion. People in Austria-Hungary didn't like that idea. So, their army moved in and completely took over Bosnia. Many Bosnians were not happy. They did not live in a free country anymore.

Serbians thought that it was wrong too. So, they came up with a plan. They heard news about Archduke Franz Ferdinand, the future ruler of the Austro-Hungarian Empire. Ferdinand was going to visit Bosnia with his wife.

A List of Demands

When Austro-Hungarian leaders made their list of demands, they knew Serbian leaders would say no. They thought it would force a war that they could win. Many leaders around the world agreed with Serbian leaders and thought the demands were too harsh.

A Second Attempt

The assassination of Archduke Ferdinand was the second attempt on his life that day. Earlier, a bomb was thrown at his car, but it hit the car behind him. People in that car were injured by the blast. Ferdinand and his wife changed their plans and were going to the hospital to see the victims of the bombing. On the way, their driver turned down a wrong street and was attempting to turn the car around when Gavrilo Princip (shown above) shot and killed them both.

On June 28, 1914, a Serbian man living in Bosnia took action. He shot and killed Ferdinand and his wife. Austro-Hungarian leaders were furious. They blamed Serbia for the **murders**. Serbian leaders swore they had nothing to do with the plan. So, Austria-Hungary made a list of demands for Serbia. The demands were extreme. Serbian leaders said they could not accept them. Within a month, Austria-Hungary declared war on Serbia.

This drawing of the death of Archduke Ferdinand appeared on the front page of European newspapers.

Choosing Sides

Austria-Hungary was not going to war alone. They had an **alliance** with Germany and Italy. That group was called the Triple Alliance. On the other side, Serbia was allies with Russia. Russia had its own alliance with Great Britain and France, called the Triple Entente. All these countries had agreed to protect one another. That meant that if any of the countries in their alliance were attacked, the other two would join the fight.

▲ This postcard shows members of the Triple Entente—France, Russia, and Great Britain.

division of Europe by the end of August 1914 ▶

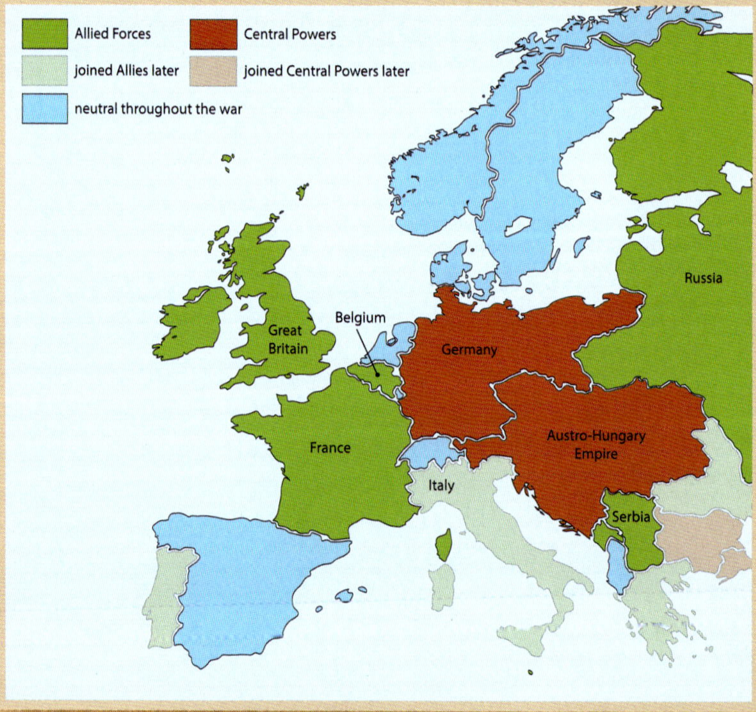

Germany quickly sided with its Triple Alliance partner, Austria-Hungary. German leaders thought that Russia and France would choose Serbia's side in the war. So, Germany decided to march through Belgium and attack France first. However, Belgium was a **neutral** country. So the German invasion was **illegal**.

Even though Great Britain was in an alliance with Russia, British leaders had planned on staying out of the war. However, that changed when Germany marched through Belgium. After that, Great Britain entered the war.

By mid-August 1914, the two sides were clear. Germany and Austria-Hungary were on one side. They were called the Central Powers. On the other side were Great Britain, France, and Russia. They were known as the Allied forces, or the Allies. Leaders in the United States felt that this war only affected Europe. They chose to stay out of it.

WAR EXTRA! The Evening World. WAR EXTRA!

"Circulation Books Open to All"

PRICE ONE CENT. NEW YORK, SATURDAY, AUGUST 1, 1914. 10 PAGES PRICE ONE CENT.

GERMANY DECLARES WAR; ALL EUROPE IS IN ARMS

ST. PETERSBURG, Aug. 1—The German Ambassador, in the name of his Government, sent to the Russian Minister of Foreign Affairs at 7.30 o'clock a declaration of war.

The announcement is made by the St. Petersburg telegraph agency, which is considered the official news agency of Russia.

RATE DECISION PROVES PARTIAL VICTORY FOR 52 EASTERN RAILROADS

WILL ADD TO INCOMES.

BANKERS CONFER TO KEEP AMERICAN GOLD AT HOME

ATLANTIC LINERS PARALYZED IN RUSH FOR PASSAGE

English Liners Refuse to Take Any Passengers for Continental Europe.

BASEBALL

NATIONAL LEAGUE

AMERICAN LEAGUE

ITALY BREAKS THE TRIPLE ALLIANCE; FRANCE CALLS OUT HER WAR ARMY

7,474,000 ANSWER FIRST CALL; 7 WARRING NATIONS CAN PUT 32,541,000 MEN IN THE FIELD

England Gives Formal Notice That She Will Side With France and Russia and Back Up Her Agreements to the Full Extent of Her Power and Resources.

▲ Headlines like this appeared around the world.

Italy Joins the War

In the years before the war, Italy's goals had moved away from the goals of the Triple Alliance. When war broke out, Italy refused to join the Central Powers. That formally ended the alliance. At first, Italy stayed neutral. Then, in April 1915, Allied leaders promised to give Italy land if the Allies won. One month later, Italy joined the Allies and declared war on its former partners in the Triple Alliance.

Joining the Ranks

Flora Sandes was a British nurse who wanted to fight in the war. The Serbian army let her join as a soldier. Before long, Sandes was promoted to sergeant major. She was wounded by a grenade blast during the war. When she recovered, she went back to fighting.

The Early Battles

At first, the war was fought on two **fronts**. The Western Front was made up of battles that took place west of Germany. The Central Powers hoped to win the Western Front quickly. However, early on, the Allies had a major victory. At the First Battle of the Marne in September 1914, the Allies stopped German troops from reaching Paris, France. Germany was forced to **retreat**.

▲ ammunition left after the First Battle of the Marne

Trench Warfare

Long ago, enemies faced each other on flat battlefields. By the early 1900s, that no longer happened. German soldiers dug the first trenches of the war. A typical trench was about 10 feet (3 meters) deep. This protected soldiers from enemy bullets.

A Deadly Battle

In 1916, the longest battle of the Western Front was fought. German troops launched an attack against the French in a battle near Verdun, France. The battle took over 10 months to complete. In that time, an estimated one million soldiers were killed or wounded.

▼ panorama taken after the Battle of Verdun

▼ Around 15,000 Russian soldiers are taken prisoner by the German army after the Tannenberg campaign.

Battlefields east of Germany were part of the Eastern Front. The Central Powers had early victories there. One of those wins came in August 1914 at a battle during the Tannenberg campaign. After five days of fighting, the Russian side had more than 125,000 **casualties**.

In late 1914, the Ottoman Empire joined the Central Powers. They quickly attacked Russia. Allied troops tried to fight back in the Battle of Gallipoli (guh-LIP-uh-lee). This was one of the bloodiest battles of the war. The Allies greatly outnumbered the Central Powers. It should have been a quick win. Together, both sides had more than 250,000 casualties. Facing such a huge loss, the Allies turned back. It was an embarrassing defeat for Allied leaders.

Growing Fronts

As the war continued, the style of fighting changed. Battles on the Western Front were primarily fought from trenches. By the end of the war, trenches stretched from the coast of Belgium to the border of Switzerland. Between the trenches were large open fields that were usually covered in barbed wire. These open fields became known as *no-man's land*. When soldiers tried to cross no-man's land, most were quickly shot down. Troops fighting on the Western Front were largely locked in a **stalemate**. That stalemate would last for most of the war.

On the Eastern Front, troops often had to travel long distances between battles. Trench warfare did not make sense there. When trenches *were* dug, they were broken quickly. Massive armies on both sides kept moving instead of staying in trenches.

This photograph of an explosion in no-man's land shows the reality of war. ▶

On both fronts, the first few years of the war did not go well for the Allies. Germany seemed unstoppable. German soldiers had taken over most of Belgium and large parts of France. From 1915 to 1917, Germany took over Poland and parts of Russia too. The Allies needed help if they were going to win the war.

▲ Allied soldiers launch gas at German troops.

More Join In

Bulgaria joined the Central Powers. Japan and Belgium joined the Allies. U.S. President Woodrow Wilson hoped to keep the United States out of the war. Still, at least 40,000 Americans joined Canada's troops. They fought for Great Britain in the war.

Modern Warfare

In 1903, brothers Orville and Wilbur Wright had completed the first ever controlled airplane flight near Kitty Hawk, North Carolina. By World War I, planes had developed enough to be used in war. World War I was also the first war to use chemicals, such as poisons, gases, and acids, to kill and injure people. Soldiers on both sides carried gas masks as protection. The first use of deadly chemicals took place in 1916. German troops threw **chlorine gas** toward French soldiers in trenches. More than ten thousand French soldiers died in only 10 minutes.

America Joins the War

As the war stretched into its third year, the United States was still officially neutral. President Wilson had been clear that he would not take sides in Europe's war. He had worked toward peace. For a few years, he succeeded.

In February 1915, German leaders declared that their navy would attack all boats in waters surrounding Great Britain. They wanted to stop boats that were bringing weapons to British troops. However, this attack plan would endanger U.S. ships in British waters that had nothing to do with the war. Germany's plan was called **unrestricted** submarine warfare.

U-boats

German submarines were very successful in the war. They were called U-boats. The nickname came from *unterseeboot*, meaning "undersea boat" in German. At the beginning of the war, Germany had 38 U-boats. By the end of the war, they had 334 U-boats!

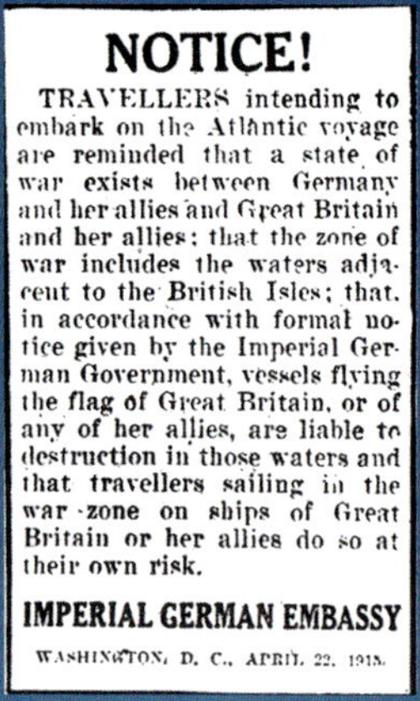

NOTICE!

TRAVELLERS intending to embark on the Atlantic voyage are reminded that a state of war exists between Germany and her allies and Great Britain and her allies; that the zone of war includes the waters adjacent to the British Isles; that, in accordance with formal notice given by the Imperial German Government, vessels flying the flag of Great Britain, or of any of her allies, are liable to destruction in those waters and that travellers sailing in the war zone on ships of Great Britain or her allies do so at their own risk.

IMPERIAL GERMAN EMBASSY

WASHINGTON, D. C., APRIL 22, 1915.

Losing the *Lusitania*

In April, Germany ran a warning in a U.S. newspaper. It said that people who sailed through British waters did so "at their own risk." Naval leaders in England also issued a warning. They asked the *Lusitania*'s captain to change course every few minutes to avoid attacks. However, the ship's captain chose to ignore this advice.

On May 1, 1915, a British ship called the *Lusitania* set sail from New York. Six days later, the *Lusitania* was nearing England when the ship was rocked. A German submarine had torpedoed the ship! The ship sank in minutes. Almost two thousand passengers aboard died. Many Americans were very angry. They told President Wilson to take action. Still, he stuck to his plan to stay out of the war.

Then, in August, a German submarine sunk a second ship with Americans onboard. Americans were **outraged**. Germany did not want the United States to enter the war. So, they agreed to stop using unrestricted submarine warfare.

As soon as Germany stopped attacking U.S. ships, many Americans backed off their desire to join the war. Throughout 1916, President Wilson kept working with both sides to end the war. He was also running for a second term as president. His campaign slogan was "He kept us out of the war." In November, Wilson was re-elected. In January of the next year, he spoke to the U.S. Senate. He said he was working for a peaceful end to the war.

By 1917, the Central Powers were firmly winning the war. This was due in part to the large German army. German leaders felt like they were unstoppable. So, in February, they changed their plans. They began using unrestricted submarine warfare again. After that, President Wilson broke off peace talks with Germany.

This truck encouraged voters to re-elect Wilson.

At the same time, British leaders **intercepted** a coded telegram to Mexico. The message was sent from a German official named Arthur Zimmermann. In it, he asked Mexico to join the war. He promised to give U.S. land to Mexico when they won. The Zimmermann Telegram, as it came to be called, made President Wilson angry. On April 6, 1917, the United States joined the Allies in the war.

▲ This 1917 political cartoon shows Germany carving up the United States.

Pershing's Past

American General John J. Pershing led the first U.S. troops to Europe. Before the war, Pershing had led troops in the Spanish-American War. In that war, all of the soldiers under Pershing's command were African American. At the time, they were one of the only all-black units in the U.S. Army.

The Zimmermann Telegram

Zimmermann knew that if President Wilson found out about the contents of the telegram, he would be mad. However, Zimmermann was willing to take that risk. He thought that even if the United States joined the war, they would not be able to organize fast enough to change the outcome. Zimmermann ended the note by saying that England would be forced "to make peace in a few months."

The Harlem Hellfighters

U.S. troops were a welcome sight for the tired Allies. They looked like a strong, united force. However, they were really not a united group. The U.S. Army was **segregated** at this time. Black and white soldiers did not serve in the same units. They held different jobs. Most black soldiers were not allowed to fight. Instead, they worked unloading ships, building transport lines, and digging graves.

The 396th Infantry Regiment was an all-black unit. They asked General Pershing to let them fight on the **front lines**. He agreed to let them serve as support for the French army.

The unit quickly earned a reputation as fierce fighters. German soldiers began calling them "hellfighters." Since the members of the 396th were all from New York, this nickname later became the Harlem Hellfighters.

▼ Harlem Hellfighters with Croix de Guerre medals in 1919

The Harlem Hellfighters served on the front lines for more than six months in 1918. That is longer than any other U.S. unit in the war. The entire unit was awarded the *Croix de Guerre* (KRAW duh GARE). That is the highest medal a French soldier can receive. Members of the unit also earned 170 additional medals for bravery. The Harlem Hellfighters became one of the most **decorated** American regiments in the war.

▼ Johnson stands in a car with other Harlem Hellfighters during a parade after the war.

Freedom in France

The French army was not segregated. When the Harlem Hellfighters fought with the French, they were treated with respect. They had one month to learn the French language, weapons, and plans. After that, they were sent to their first post, which turned out to be 191 consecutive days on the front lines.

Young Heroes

On May 15, 1918, at least 12 German soldiers attacked a guard post. Hellfighters Henry Johnson (shown above) and Needham Roberts were on duty that night. Johnson received 21 wounds in the fight. Even injured, he still stopped the soldiers from taking Roberts as a prisoner. Stories like these made their way into U.S. news. When the Hellfighters returned home, many people treated them like heroes.

The Home Front

Back in the United States, President Wilson knew that he needed more soldiers for the war. In May, he started a **draft**. By law, all men between the ages of 21 and 35 had to register for the draft. The draft worked—by the end of the war, the U.S. Army had 20 times more soldiers than it did before the war.

President Wilson wanted nonsoldiers to help in the war effort too. He encouraged Americans to buy Liberty bonds. These were loans that Americans gave to the government to pay for the war. Wilson also formed the Committee on Public Information. They spread anti-German **propaganda**. For the most part, these methods worked. Communities came together to oppose Germany and support the war. People on the home front sent money, food, and clothing to help soldiers.

The Russian Revolution

Just as the United States entered the war, another major power left. By 1917, almost two million Russian soldiers had died in the war. The Russian leader—Tsar Nicholas II—forced men to join. Among the soldiers were farmers. With fewer farmers, there was less food, and people began to starve. Tsar Nicholas was forced to step down, and a new group seized power. Their leader—Vladimir Lenin—quickly withdrew Russia from the war. By the time they left, three-fourths of Russia's soldiers had been wounded, killed, taken prisoner, or were missing.

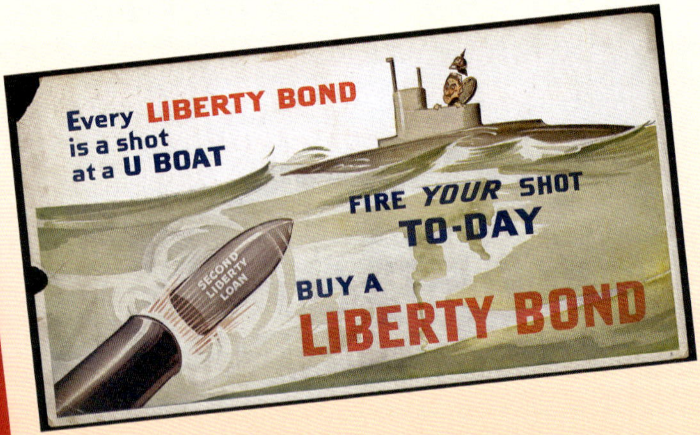

▲ 1917 poster for Liberty bonds

Men hold their draft registration cards in June 1917.

Not everyone supported the war, and around three million men refused to serve. They either did not register for the draft or did not show up when they were called. These men became known as *draft dodgers*. U.S. newspapers called draft dodgers "cowards" and "slackers." Some draft dodgers were caught and sent to jail. Others moved to Canada to avoid jail time.

A group of women speak out against the draft in New York in June 1917.

The End of the War

In early 1918, the outcome of the war looked good for the Central Powers. Russia had pulled all its troops out of the war. Only 85,000 U.S. soldiers had made it to France by March. German troops were close to capturing Paris, France. And on the Western Front, there were more soldiers from Germany than all the Allied countries combined.

Then, U.S. troops began arriving in huge numbers. Nearly 10,000 U.S. soldiers arrived each day. By September, there were 1.2 million U.S. soldiers in France. They were newly trained and well supplied. The U.S. Navy also sent hundreds of ships to destroy the German navy. These movements gave hope to the Allies.

▼ **Americans show headlines announcing the end of the war.**

At the same time, the once-unstoppable German troops were getting weaker. Allied **blockades** stopped food from reaching Germany. People there were starving. They begged the government to stop the war so the blockades would end.

By July, the Allies had taken control of the war. Germany launched one last attack at the Second Battle of the Marne. However, the Allies had pushed Germany back by early August. In September, some Central Powers surrendered. Bulgaria was first. Then came the Austro-Hungarians and the Ottomans. On November 11, German leaders agreed to stop fighting.

After four long, bloody years, the Allies had won the war.

Skilled Women

Over 13,000 women joined the military during the war. Most were nurses or "Hello Girls." Hello Girls were switchboard operators. Without Hello Girls, most phone calls took about one minute to connect. Hello Girls could connect phone calls in about 10 seconds. They had to know both English and French so they could translate any calls they received. They helped pass information between leaders. Hello Girls were among the first Americans sent to the war. They were also among the last to leave as they helped translate peace talks.

After Germany agreed to stop fighting, the Allied leaders had to discuss what would happen next. In January 1919, the major Allied leaders met in France. They began work on a peace **treaty**. The treaty said Germany could keep a small army and navy. Germany would have to give money to the Allies. That money would help pay for all the damage that the war had caused. The treaty also started the League of Nations. This group was President Wilson's idea. The League of Nations would settle problems between countries. People hoped that it would prevent future wars.

German and Allied leaders signed the Treaty of Versailles (ver-SIGH) on June 28, 1919. However, the U.S. Senate would not agree to the treaty. Part of joining the League of Nations meant the United States would have to send troops to help any League member in any war. Many senators did not like that the United States might be forced into wars. They would not sign the treaty until that part was removed. Wilson tried to defend the treaty, but it did not work. In March 1920, the U.S. Senate finally dropped the treaty. It was never **ratified** by the United States. The United States also did not join the League of Nations.

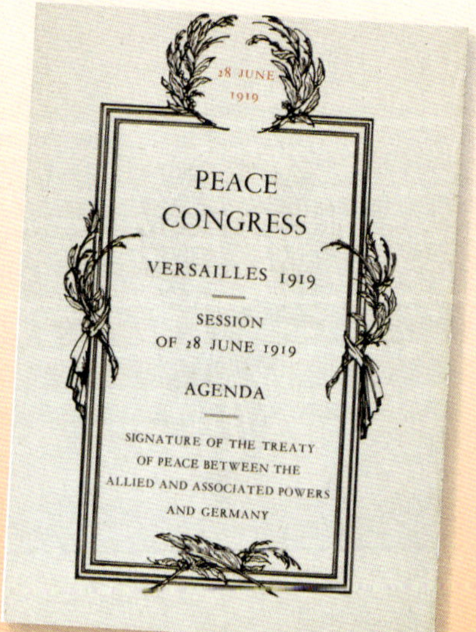
28 JUNE
1919

PEACE
CONGRESS

VERSAILLES 1919

SESSION
OF 28 JUNE 1919

AGENDA

SIGNATURE OF THE TREATY
OF PEACE BETWEEN THE
ALLIED AND ASSOCIATED POWERS
AND GERMANY

Wilson's Defense

Wilson was a strong believer in the League of Nations. He traveled around the country giving speeches about its merits. In three weeks, Wilson gave 37 speeches in 29 cities. He was exhausted and eventually collapsed after a speech. Wilson returned to the White House. A few days later, he suffered a **stroke**. Wilson slowly improved, but he never fully recovered.

The League of Nations

Even without the United States, the League of Nations moved forward. Over 60 countries joined. For years, the League settled problems. However, by the 1930s, it was growing weaker. After being unable to stop World War II, the League of Nations was replaced by a new group—the United Nations.

▼ This 1919 painting shows world leaders signing the Treaty of Versailles. President Wilson is in the middle holding papers.

The Impact of the War

After four years of fighting, more than 8 million soldiers were dead. Nearly 30 million more had been injured, taken prisoner, or were missing. Allied leaders blamed Germany entirely for the war. A lot of people felt this was not fair. The harsh terms of the Treaty of Versailles left many German people angry with the Allies.

Former German colonies in Africa and Asia came under Allied control. The Ottoman Empire was divided. So was the Austro-Hungarian Empire. New, smaller states formed. British leaders thought Jewish people should have their own homeland. Britain offered land taken from Palestine for this purpose. Many Jewish people moved there after the war. This was the first step to creating the modern country of Israel. To this day, Palestinians and Israelis fight over control of this land.

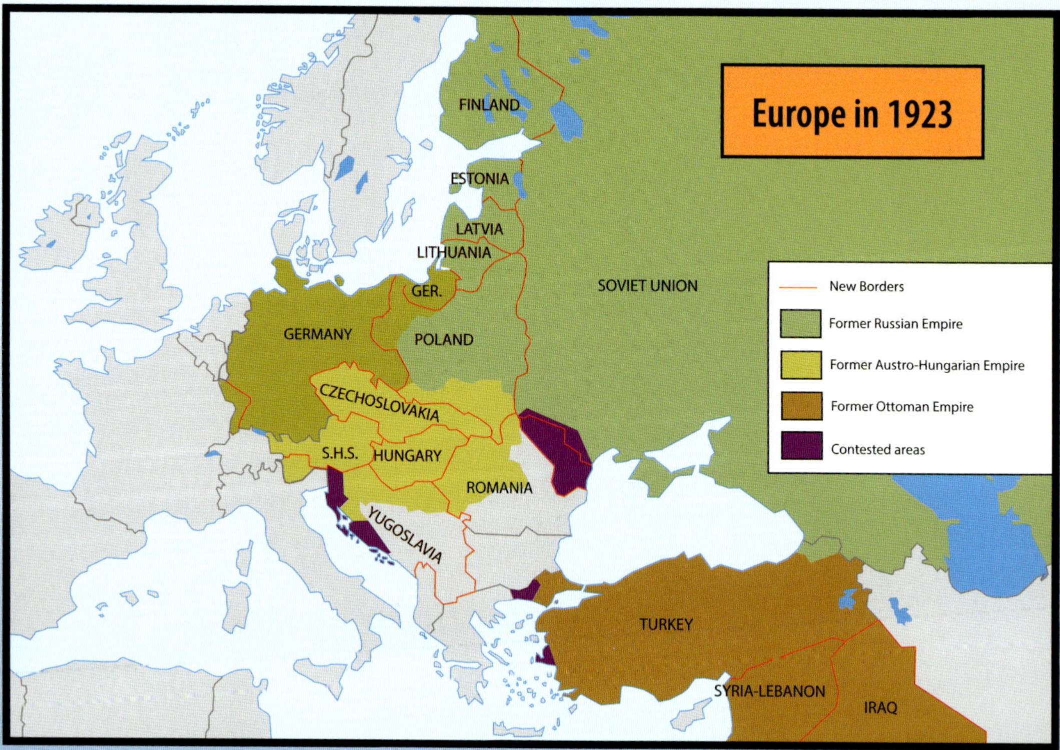

The soldiers who fought in World War I thought they were fighting a war to end all wars. They thought it would never be forgotten because it was so important. However, many people do not know much about this war. Another worldwide war—World War II—became much more well-known. For this reason, World War I is sometimes called the Forgotten War. Even though people may have forgotten it, World War I forever changed the world.

Russian doctors help wounded German soldiers during World War I. ▼

Adolf Hitler

A German soldier named Adolf Hitler fought in World War I. After the war, Hitler rose to power in Germany. He spoke out against the Treaty of Versailles. Hitler became the leader of Germany in 1934. His actions began World War II in 1939.

Wilson's Peace

President Wilson thought the terms of the Treaty of Versailles were too severe. He did not think Germany should have to pay for the war and accept all the blame. However, British and French leaders overruled him. Wilson won the Nobel Peace Prize in 1919. Wilson was awarded the prize partly for his role in forming the League of Nations.

Code It!

When the Zimmermann Telegram was intercepted, it was written completely in code. It was up to British cryptographers to find out what it meant. *Cryptographers* are people who create and solve codes and coded language. The Zimmermann Telegram had a very complex code. It took cryptographers a whole month to crack the code of the single telegram.

Create your own coded message! Write about an important event from World War I. Then, change your message into a coded message. Exchange messages with a friend. See if you can crack their code!

Examples of Codes

What You Mean	What You Write
a	1
b	2
c	3

What You Mean	What You Write
a	b
b	c
c	d

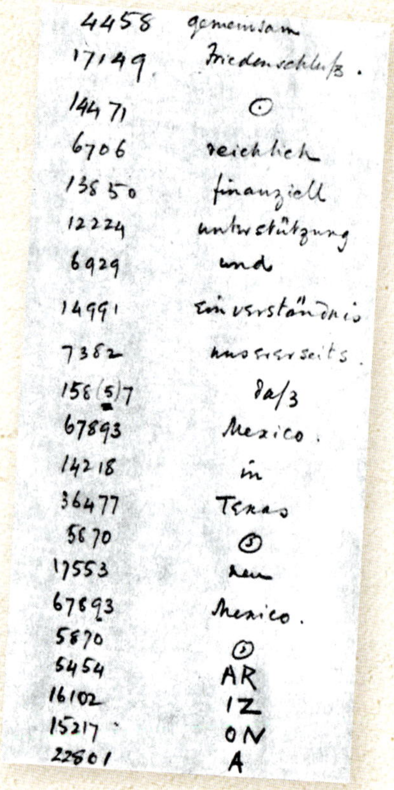
4458 gemeinsam
17149 Friedensschluß.
14471
6706 reichlich
13850 finanziell
12224 unterstützung
6929 und
14991 Einverständnis
7382 unsererseits.
158(5)7 daß
67893 Mexico.
14218 in
36477 Texas
5670
17553 neu
67893 Mexico.
5870
5454 AR
16102 IZ
15217 ON
22801 A

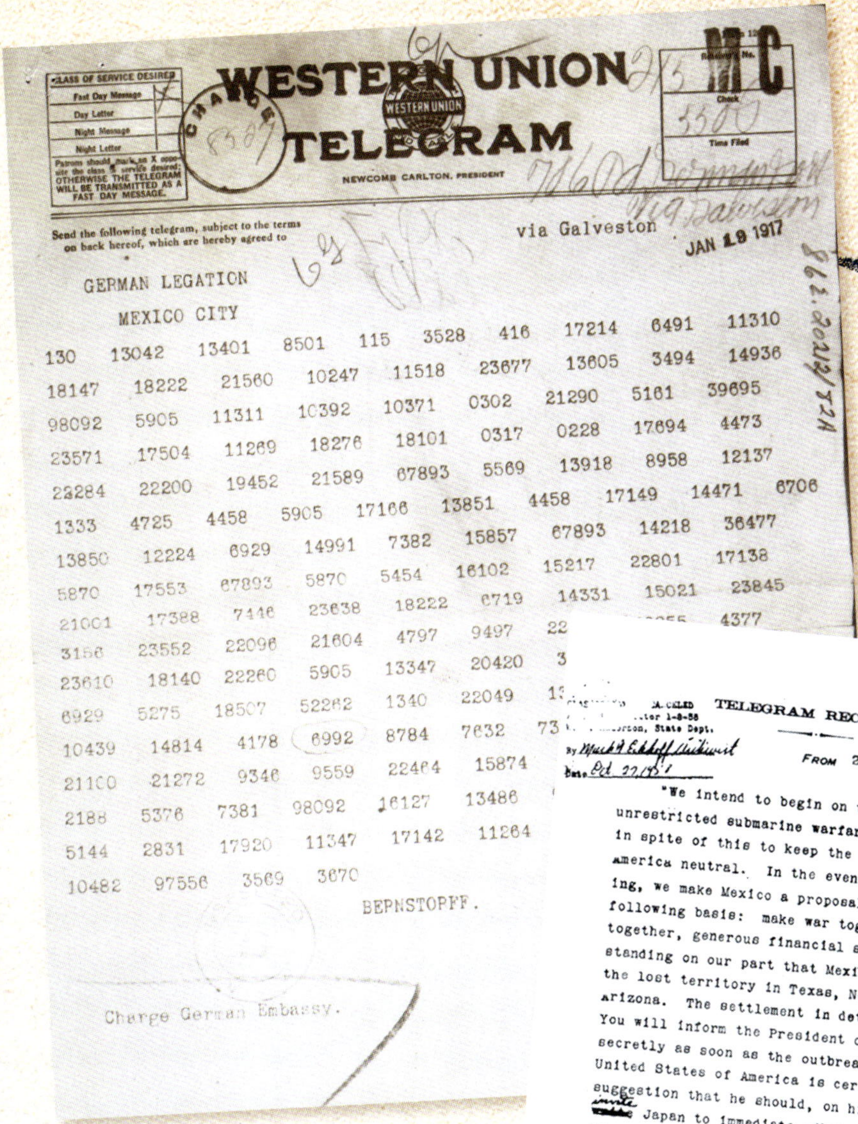
WESTERN UNION TELEGRAM

NEWCOMB CARLTON, PRESIDENT

CLASS OF SERVICE DESIRED
Fast Day Message
Day Letter
Night Message
Night Letter
Patrons should mark an X opposite the class of service desired; OTHERWISE THE TELEGRAM WILL BE TRANSMITTED AS A FAST DAY MESSAGE.

Send the following telegram, subject to the terms on back hereof, which are hereby agreed to

via Galveston JAN 19 1917

GERMAN LEGATION

MEXICO CITY

130 13042 13401 8501 115 3528 416 17214 6491 11310
18147 18222 21560 10247 11518 23677 13605 3494 14936
98092 5905 11311 10392 10371 0302 21290 5161 39695
23571 17504 11269 18276 18101 0317 0228 17694 4473
23284 22200 19452 21589 67893 5569 13918 8958 12137
1333 4725 4458 5905 17166 13851 4458 17149 14471 6706
13850 12224 6929 14991 7382 15857 67893 14218 36477
5870 17553 67893 5870 5454 16102 15217 22801 17138
21001 17388 7446 23638 18222 6719 14331 15021 23845
3156 23552 22096 21604 4797 9497 22 4377
23610 18140 22260 5905 13347 20420 3
6929 5275 18507 52262 1340 22049 1
10439 14814 4178 6992 8784 7632 73
21100 21272 9346 9559 22464 15874
2188 5376 7381 98092 16127 13486
5144 2831 17920 11347 17142 11264
10482 97556 3569 3670

BERNSTORFF.

Charge German Embassy.

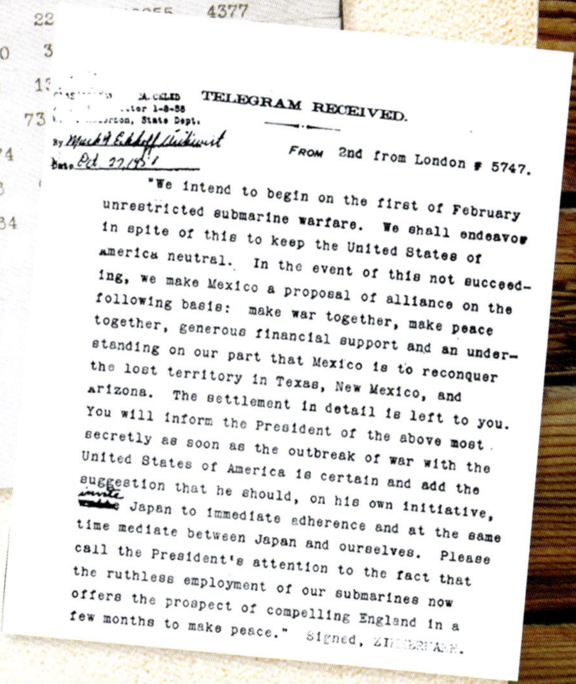
TELEGRAM RECEIVED.

FROM 2nd from London # 5747.

"We intend to begin on the first of February unrestricted submarine warfare. We shall endeavor in spite of this to keep the United States of America neutral. In the event of this not succeeding, we make Mexico a proposal of alliance on the following basis: make war together, make peace together, generous financial support and an understanding on our part that Mexico is to reconquer the lost territory in Texas, New Mexico, and Arizona. The settlement in detail is left to you. You will inform the President of the above most secretly as soon as the outbreak of war with the United States of America is certain and add the suggestion that he should, on his own initiative, invite Japan to immediate adherence and at the same time mediate between Japan and ourselves. Please call the President's attention to the fact that the ruthless employment of our submarines now offers the prospect of compelling England in a few months to make peace." Signed, ZIMMERMANN.

Glossary

alliance—close association of nations or other groups

blockades—acts of war in which soldiers or ships are used to stop people and supplies from entering or leaving places

casualties—people who are killed, captured, or seriously injured during warfare

chlorine gas—a type of gas that causes difficulty breathing and may cause vomiting and death

decorated—given medals or awards

draft—a selection of people from the general population for military service

front lines—areas in wars where a lot of fighting takes place

fronts—areas where active warfare are taking place

illegal—against rules or laws

intercepted—seized or took something before it could arrive at its planned destination

murders—the killing of people

neutral—not connected to or supporting either side of a fight, an argument, or a war

outraged—feeling extreme anger

propaganda—statements or ideas that are often exaggerated or false and are spread to help a cause

ratified—made official by signing it or voting for it

retreat—to move away from the threat of danger or attack

segregated—separated by race, religion, or other factors

stalemate—a situation in which neither side can gain an advantage or a win

stroke—a serious illness caused when a blood vessel in the brain suddenly breaks or is blocked

treaty—an official agreement made between two or more countries or groups

unrestricted—not limited or controlled in any way

Index

Your Turn!

When the United States entered the war, President Wilson knew it would be very expensive. He decided to raise money to help pay for the war through the sale of Liberty bonds. Liberty bonds were investments that people made in the U.S. government. People gave the government money to spend in the war. Then, after the war was over, the government paid back the money plus interest. Liberty bonds were sold in a wide range of values to make sure that all men, women, and children could afford them.

This photograph shows a famous movie actor, Douglas Fairbanks, encouraging people in New York City to buy Liberty bonds in April 1918. Imagine you are Fairbanks. What can you say to convince the crowd to buy Liberty bonds? Write a speech for Fairbanks. Then, deliver your speech with enthusiasm and energy.